DASH Gordon

by

Renne' Siewers

Dash Gordon dedicates this book
to special needs, autism,
human trafficking, veterans,
domestic violence and abuse,
and foster children
and their families.

Dash Gordon's information is on
his Facebook page and
on the website

thedashgordonfoundation.org

or infothedashgordonfoundation.org.

Illustrations by Renne' Siewers

Especially dedicated to
Dash Supporter(s):

_____

From:_____

Tommy said, "I'm hungry. I want Dash Gordon to bring me a pizza." Mom said, "I'll call Dash immediately. He'll bring your pizza and make you smile."

Dash answered the urgent call
saying, "I'll pick up the pizza
and Dash right over."
Dash put on his Dash Gordon suit
and picked up the pizza
for little Tommy.

Dash delivered the pizza to
Little Tommy. Dash Gordon
gave little Tommy a big smile,
and they both laughed.

He texts on his phone and writes everyone about how to get help in the neighborhood when needed.

Dash organized the Winter Formal

for all the special needs

teenagers in the area.

So many generous people

volunteered their help,

decorations, and hall to make this

a memorable night.

Dash was the DJ

selecting the music.

To create memories, these two
take pictures to remember
the Winter Formal.

Two girlfriends enjoy the evening with music, food, and dance. They danced the night away.

Dash Gordon to the rescue! Zoom!
He is only interested in giving
to people that need him
or need help.

Dash hopes to make the world a better and kinder place.

Zoom!!!

Zoom!!! First, he drives to
Sanctuary Foster Care Services.
He sees a boy and girl leaving for
a new home with new parents.
These new parents want to
take care of a special child.

The children love
Dash Gordon's outfit
and jovial smile.

Dash says to everyone,
"Give a child a loving home,
in addition to your family,
making the children secure
and hopeful for a better life and
stability. Only you can step up
to the responsibility
of a child's dreams.
Foster a child in need."

Making a child happy creates love inside your heart. So, fill your heart with joy.

Next, he goes to a place called
Mady's Movement.
Dash meets Nicole Bowie,
founder, and mother of Mady.
Someone took Mady from
her Mom. Mady didn't know
about bad people who do
bad things, whether someone
you know or Stranger Danger.
She was only a teenager and
should have listened to her Mom.
Dash says,
"If you see something,
say something."

**Dash says,
"Protect our children!"**

Next, Dash Gordon spends
the afternoon at
Rainbow of Hope. Zoom!!!
There he visits
extraordinary people with
developmental issues.
He talks to them about their
social skills. Social skills are
when you say, "Thank You",
"Yes Sir", "No Sir", or knowing
when to speak to others.
In addition, Rainbow of Hope
teaches life skills like
using a checkbook, cooking,
or even riding a horse.

You, too, could learn to be
an awesome Chef or
cook for yourself or your family.

Joey told Mommy and Daddy,

"Watch me ride the horse!"

Daddy said, in a relaxed,

peaceful environment,

"I like you having a routine."

Dash Gordon said,

"Enjoy every minute

with your family."

Dash waves to Joey as

she rode the beautiful horse,

Lady Hope,

away from the sun.

**Dash shouts,
"Have a safe horseback ride."**

Sarah's House

Dash is on the way. Zoom!!!
Clara said, "Dash, I don't know
where to go. I don't have
food or a place to stay
for my daughter and me."
Dash came to her rescue,
"I know the perfect place."
Dash called Sarah's House,
"They will help you begin again
at Sarah's House. They will give
you shelter, clothes, and food."
Clara cried joyfully, "Thank you,
Dash, you are a lifesaver.
I didn't know what to do.
Now I can sleep in peace tonight. "

Dash said,
"Sleep, baby girl, sleep
with beautiful dreams."

As Dash drives away, you can hear his happiness in planning how he will help the next person

My Hero, Dash Gordon

Once upon a time, a man delivered food for Dash.

He went to the children's homes traveling so fast.

He dashed to their door

And came in with a roar

Making all the children giggle

With his smiles and wiggles

Dash is a true hero

Bringing joy high and low

To all kinds of people who need help now

Around the town, he gives them hope with a pow

May Dash Gordon continue providing

To everyone who needs a new beginning

Go, my hero, Dash Gordon

Renne' Siewers

Coloring Pages

Look for **other children's books online:**

Nighty Night Sailboat
(sailing terms)
Noche Noche Velero
(bilingual Spanish/English - sailing terms)
Nighty Night Sailboat Goes to Spain
(Spanish culture - provision a boat)
Santa finds Nighty Night Sailboat
(Children who move or may not be home for Christmas)
Nighty Night Sailboat in the Bahamas
(Bahamian culture – going through customs)
Nighty Night Sailboat Celebrates Key West Birthday
(What to do in Key West - making new friends)
Nighty Night Sailboat Searches for Pirates
(History of Blackbeard – Bullies)
Sailing Angels Crew for Nighty Night Sailboat
(Doing a Good Deed)
Nighty Night Sailboat takes Juni to the Hospital
(What to expect at a hospital or doctor's office.)
Nighty Night Sailboat Meets an Astronaut
(Spin-off technologies)
Piggish Birthday
(Making life better.)

Check out Amazon
or
Do A REVIEW:
https://www.amazon.com/review/create-review?ie=UTF8&asin =
www.sailadybooks.blogspot.com

Made in the USA
Columbia, SC
11 March 2023

13652021R00018